Beyond Expectations

The Extraordinary power of
Satisfying Customers More Than
They Expect

Abraham Scott

© **Abraham Scott, 2024.** All rights reserved. Except for brief quotations included in critical reviews and certain other noncommercial uses allowed by copyright law, no part of this book may be reproduced, distributed, or transmitted in any form or by any means, including photocopying, recording, or other electronic or mechanical methods, without the publisher's prior written permission.

Table of content

Introduction   6
   The Influence of Exceeding Expectations   6
Chapter One   12
   Consumer Expectations   12
Chapter Two   20
   The Consumer Expectation Psychology   20
Chapter Three   25
   Establishing an Exceptional Service Culture 25
Chapter Four   34
   Recognising Needs of Customers   34
Chapter Five   56
   The Little Things That Makes A Big Difference   56
Chapter Six   82
   Going Above and Beyond   82
Chapter Seven   89
   Using Complaints to Create Chances   89
Chapter Eight   96
   Assessing and Enhancing Client Satisfaction

96
Chapter Nine   **104**
   Using Technology to Provide Better Service 104
Chapter Ten   **113**
   Staying Ahead of Industry Trends   113
Chapter Eleven   **128**
   Case Studies and Success Stories   128
   Customer Service's Future   128
Conclusion   **138**
   Final Thoughts   138
Acknowledgement   **144**

Introduction

The Influence of Exceeding Expectations

Businesses often look for ways to differentiate themselves from the competition and gain the trust of their clientele in today's cutthroat market. Going above and above for customers is one of the most effective ways to accomplish this. This goes beyond just providing for your clients' necessities; it also entails surprising and satisfying them in ways they never would have imagined.

When a company goes beyond and above what is anticipated, it leaves a lasting impression that builds trust and stronger emotional ties. This strategy turns infrequent consumers into passionate supporters who not only come back but also tell others about their wonderful experiences.

Knowing and foreseeing your consumers' unsaid needs is the key to exceeding their expectations.

Every action we do in both our personal and professional lives is accompanied by expectations. Everybody remembers growing up with expectations like doing their homework, taking a bath, brushing their teeth, and finishing their chores. There are demands from employers, coaches, instructors, and parents. When we live up to those expectations, people are content. They become unhappy if we don't, and an awkward conversation usually ensues.

There isn't a secret recipe. There's only one thing to do: claw, grind, and work your way up to the point where you surpass your clients' and customers' expectations. I am aware that neither as an individual nor as an entrepreneur, any magic bullets brought me to where I am now.

It's no secret that a lot of us try to justify our failures. But to be a successful business leader, you must do something that sets you apart from your rivals and gives your clients and consumers the impression that you appreciate them more than the rival company down the street. Once more, this isn't a secret recipe; rather, it's a technique I adopted to differentiate myself: going above and beyond for them.

You should be aware that there is more rivalry than ever in the business world nowadays as an entrepreneur. Providing a high-quality good or service is now insufficient. You must surpass expectations. Think about this instance: You and your friends are playing games over the weekend, but the internet isn't working. When you contact your service provider, the issue is not being resolved quickly. Your pals want you to return and place an order for dinner because it has been over an hour. You can't call it in at this time since you are on the phone. But after 20 minutes, you hear the doorbell, and the internet service agent hears this and places a pizza order on your behalf.

Now what do you do? You might post about your experience on social media because you're so impressed. What was the internet provider's cost of this? Perhaps $20? In exchange, it gains a devoted client and might even receive free advertising in the form of a client endorsement.

Numerous instances exist of little actions taken by major corporations that have a global impact on people's lives. About a year ago, I came into a Cricket Wireless campaign in which the company unintentionally exposed WWE legend John Cena to the public. In part two of the campaign, Cena read out some of the fan mail he receives daily. The internet was inundated with campaign posts like wildfire.

When I give guidance to business executives, I focus mostly on these small details, and I've even ingrained them into the culture of my organization. Small gestures like giving a customer a meaningful gift or writing a handmade thank-you message make a big impression. Seek out opportunities for surprise and delight as they may serve as triggers to attract new customers and hold onto current ones.

You will realize that you are moving in the correct path if you set these tiny precedents and lay these little building stones. Together, these little pieces form a bigger whole. Recall that a river is formed by billions of individual water droplets. While one of these drops might not matter much on its own, put together they form a powerful force. Think of your tiny efforts as droplets; if you do things correctly, you will witness your organization transform into the river with greater reward and satisfaction from customer , clients or consumer

Chapter One

Consumer Expectations

What Expectations Do Consumer Have?

Consumer expectations are people's projected results, experiences, and requirements about the caliber, features, and interactions of a good or service. These expectations are shaped by several variables, such as prior encounters, marketing materials, word-of-mouth referrals, cultural influences, and individual preferences.

Consumer expectations are the standards by which consumers assess and measure their dealings with a company. These standards cover a wide range of factors, including emotional resonance, value for money, ease of use, product performance, and service dependability. If these are met or beyond, customers are more likely to be happy, become devoted, and promote the business.

Growing customer expectations are a result of shifting consumer behavior, technology improvements, and shifting market trends. They are not static. Consumers want companies to be aware of these changing expectations and to take proactive steps to match their experiences and offers with them. These companies will be in a better position to build stronger relationships with their customers and prosper in the cutthroat industry.

It is impossible to exaggerate the significance of client expectations for any size firm. Achieving sustainable development, cultivating great customer connections, and rewarding loyalty all depend on meeting and beyond these expectations. Expectations are essential for every firm to succeed for many reasons.

Higher levels of customer satisfaction are a result of meeting consumer expectations. Customers who are happy with your service are more likely to promote it to others, come back for more purchases, and write favorable reviews. On the other hand, falling short of expectations can cause discontent and bad press, which can damage your reputation.

Loyalty is cultivated when expectations are consistently met or exceeded by the customer. Even when faced with competition, devoted clients remain loyal to your brand over time. They turn into evangelists who tell their network about your goods and services, so acting as a free marketing avenue.

The reputation of your brand is influenced by customer expectations. When you regularly fulfill your commitments, people will identify your brand with dependability and credibility. In a saturated market, this good reputation can draw in new clients and set your company apart.

You can gain a competitive edge by comprehending and exceeding client expectations. Companies that deliver outstanding experiences regularly are more likely to stand out and draw clients away from rivals. This benefit is especially noteworthy in sectors where the goods and services offered are comparable.

A devoted client is more inclined to make more purchases. When customers are confident in your ability to meet their requirements and expectations, they will come back for more purchases. Revenue and profitability are greatly influenced by repeat business.

Customer attrition, or churn, is a problem that many businesses face. You may lessen the chance of losing clients to other businesses by continuously exceeding customer expectations. Your consumer base's stabilization helps you generate consistent income and see sustainable growth.

Positive experiences are more likely to be shared by content customers with friends, family, and coworkers. Recommendations from friends and family have great power and can greatly influence your efforts to attract new customers.

Innovation and improvement are driven by customer expectations and feedback. You can improve your competitive offerings by creating new features, services, or products that meet the requirements and wishes of your clients by actively listening to them.

Satisfying consumer expectations fosters a feeling of emotional bond between your company and its clients. Deeper ties and higher client lifetime value are the results of emotional connections.

Long-term business success is ultimately the result of consistently surpassing customer expectations. A stable client base and good market position are facilitated by devoted customers and positive word-of-mouth.

<u>10 Expectations from Customers/ Consumers That You Should Never Forget</u>

1. Genuineness:- Consumers look to brands for integrity and sincerity. To preserve trust and loyalty, steer clear of making exaggerated statements and make sure that all customer touchpoints are consistent.

2. Precise Expectations:- Based on brand promises, customers have particular expectations. To prevent disappointing customers, make sure your product or service lives up to the expectations you have set out.

3. Implied Expectations: These are predicated on performance criteria that have been set and industry norms. Achieving or surpassing these can have a favorable impact on consumer decisions.

4. Easy and Hassle-Free:- Consumers like easy and quick transactions. To win over customers' trust and contentment, streamline and simplify operations.

5. Humanise:- View clients as unique people with feelings and needs. Loyalty and happiness are increased through direct communication and sincere connections.

6. Steady Expectations:- Make sure that performance and quality are constant. Consumers look to you for dependable and easily accessible goods and services.

7. Evolving Expectations:- Adjust and develop over time to satisfy shifting client requirements. Updates, new features, and support are necessary to ensure long-term enjoyment.

8. Evolving Technological Expectations:- Keep up with the latest developments in technology. Consumers, particularly in tech-driven sectors, anticipate new features and advancements.

9. Keep It Simple and Easy:- Create offerings that are easy for customers to use and keep things simple throughout the customer journey, from assistance before to after the sale.

10. Ongoing Assistance:- Offer trustworthy client assistance. Customers will feel more confident in your brand if you reassure them that they will get assistance when needed.

Chapter Two

The Consumer Expectation Psychology

The study of consumers' expectations and how they change in response to different circumstances is known as the psychology of expectations. There are several psychological concepts at work which applies to consumer Expectation Psychology.

- **Expectation-Confirmation idea:** According to this idea, consumers set expectations based on preexisting notions and experiences. Satisfaction arises when the real experience meets or surpasses these expectations. If the encounter is not up to par, discontent ensues.

- **The Anchor Effect:** The "anchor" effect refers to how customers frequently base their expectations on the initial piece of information they are given. For instance, their early impressions and assessments may be influenced by the price or feature set.

- **Social Proof:** People are swayed by the insights and viewpoints of others. Social media, testimonies, and reviews can greatly influence their expectations.

- **Contrast Effect:** A customer's impression is amplified when their experience deviates dramatically from their expectations, whether in a good or negative way. Meeting or surpassing expectations can increase happiness, but falling short of them might increase dissatisfaction.

Businesses may create strategies to manage and surpass consumer expectations and increase customer satisfaction and loyalty by having a solid understanding of these psychological concepts.

Determining the Needs and Wants of Customers.

Delivering outstanding service and products requires understanding the needs and desires of the consumer.

Wants are the extras that make a customer's experience better, whereas needs are the necessities that must be met. Businesses can employ several techniques to precisely identify these through Direct client feedback obtained through surveys and questionnaires can offer valuable insights into their requirements and preferences.

It is important to craft questions that would elicit precise details about their experiences and expectations.

Interviews with clients one-on-one. These can provide more in-depth information about their preferences and problems. Feedback that is more specific and tailored is made possible by these exchanges.

Holding talks in groups with certain clients can offer a more comprehensive understanding of their needs and preferences. These discussions can reveal recurring themes and original thoughts. Recurring problems and development opportunities can be found by examining feedback from a variety of sources, such as social media comments, internet reviews, and customer service encounters.

Tracking consumer behaviors like usage and purchase trends, businesses can gain an indirect understanding of their requirements and preferences. Analytics programs and customer relationship management (CRM) platforms can be used to gather this data.

Knowing what they are delivering and how they are satisfying client needs can help you set useful standards and generate better suggestions. By integrating these techniques, companies can gain a thorough grasp of the requirements and preferences of their clients, allowing them to customize their products and continually surpass client expectations.

Chapter Three

Establishing an Exceptional Service Culture

Cultivating a Customer-First Mentality Establishing a customer-centric perspective across the entire organization is the first step toward developing a culture of great service. This entails centering all decisions, actions, and strategies on the needs of the client. To develop and maintain a customer-centric mindset, there are steps you need to follow:

Step 1: Vision and Values:- Incorporate customer-centric values into the mission and vision statements of the organization. Emphasize the significance of providing outstanding customer service as a fundamental principle.

Step 2: Communication:- Consistently convey to all staff members the significance of customer focus. To reaffirm the message, use internal communications, newsletters, and meetings.

Step 3: Insights from Customers:- Compile and disseminate customer data throughout departments. To learn about the requirements and preferences of your customers, analyze data from surveys, interactions, and customer feedback.

Step 4: Rewards and Acknowledgement:- Establish incentive schemes that pay staff members for providing outstanding customer service. Honor and commend team members who surpass expectations.

Step 5: Customer Feedback Loop:- Create systems for gathering and responding to consumer input. Utilize these comments to inform future developments and demonstrate to clients the value of their feedback.

Step 6: Empathy and Understanding:- Teach staff members to comprehend and share the perspectives of consumers. Promote attentive listening and prompt handling of client problems.

Step 7: Cross-Functional Collaboration:- Encourage departmental cooperation to guarantee a smooth client experience. Dismantle departmental silos and promote teamwork for the good of the client.

Step 8: Client-Focused KPIs:- Establish key performance indicators (KPIs) that gauge the caliber of services and client satisfaction. Make use of these measurements to promote responsibility and ongoing development.

Without inspiration and education, innovation is impossible. The lack of originality is known as stagnation, and far too many teams don't use education to keep the creative juices flowing.

Education may spur increased output, quality, and engagement in any form of team, be it a department as a whole, a small group of multitasking employees, or even a class of pupils.

An engaged team has many advantages; according to a Gallup survey, businesses that effectively engaged their employees outperformed those in the lowest quartile for engagement in terms of profitability and productivity by 22% and 21%, respectively.

Are you unsure about how to use education to engage your team? Here are seven creative methods:

Outstanding customer service requires a team that is empowered and well-trained. This is how you prepare your staff to go above and beyond for customers or consumers

Create training curricula covering product knowledge, communication techniques, and customer service ethics. Incorporate role-playing exercises to simulate real-world encounters.

Offer chances for ongoing education via webinars, workshops, and online courses. Educate the group on current market trends and recommended procedures. Give staff members the freedom to decide for themselves and take activities that will benefit the client. Give them the freedom to handle problems on their own, without constant manager approval.

Establish an atmosphere that makes staff members feel heard and appreciated. Promote open communication and offer tools for resolving issues. Provide staff members with the materials and tools they need to help clients efficiently. Make sure they have access to the most recent data and innovations.

Consistently offer employees coaching and constructive criticism to help them develop their skills. Utilise performance evaluations to pinpoint areas in need of improvement. Encourage a spirit of unity and cooperation among staff members. Plan team-building exercises that foster closer bonds and better cooperation.

Acknowledge and honor staff members who provide outstanding customer service. To inspire the team, use both official recognition programs and sincere gratitude.

To establish and uphold the highest standards for outstanding customer service, leadership is essential. Effective leaders can motivate and direct their workers to put the customer experience first. Here are some ways that leadership can promote an extraordinary service culture:

- **Lead by Example:-** Show your dedication to providing excellent customer service by your deeds and mannerisms. In every interaction, demonstrate attentiveness, empathy, and a customer-first mentality.

- **Set Clear Expectations:-** Clearly state what constitutes outstanding customer service and let the staff know what is expected of them. Give precise instances to demonstrate the desired behaviors.

- **Align Goals and Objectives:-** Put surpassing customer expectations at the center of organizational goals and objectives. Make certain that each department is aware of its responsibility in providing outstanding customer service.

- **Resource Allocation:-** Provide enough staff, money, and time to support customer service efforts. Make investments in infrastructure, technology, and training to improve the customer experience.

- **Measure and Monitor:-** Use performance metrics, surveys, and feedback to consistently gauge customer happiness and service quality. Utilize this information to monitor developments and pinpoint areas that need work.

- **Promote Accountability:-** Make staff members answerable for providing outstanding customer service. To make sure that expectations are being fulfilled, do performance evaluations and routine check-ins.

- **Support Innovation:-** Motivate staff members to devise inventive ways to improve the clientele's experience. Establish a space where fresh concepts are accepted and explored.

- **Celebrate Successes:-** Honour achievements and landmarks in the field of customer service. Give teams and individuals that contribute to great customer experiences public recognition and rewards.

A culture of excellent service that continuously surpasses customer expectations and promotes long-term success may be established inside your organization by fostering a customer-centric mindset, providing training and empowerment to your team, and utilizing strong leadership.

Chapter Four

Recognising Needs of Customers

Proactive customer service Anticipating customers' requirements and taking the initiative is the essence of proactive customer service. Acquire the skills necessary to execute it well to establish enduring relationships and trust.

proactive client support Company trust is at an all-time low. According to the State of Consumer Data Privacy Survey, only 21% of customers have faith in international brands to protect their data. Given the increase in data breaches, spam, and data privacy issues, it makes sense that people don't trust businesses; after all, they usually assume the worst.

Companies have to look for ways to be proactive in their customer care rather than just reactive if they want to gain the trust of their customers.

For a business to succeed, proactive customer service is essential.

Anticipating customers' wants (or problems) before they become aware of them or need to get in touch with you for help is known as proactive customer service. Proactive support examples include: Notifying clients right once of errors or problems, such as service outages and shipment delays. Introducing potential consumers to new goods and services. Searching out methods to enhance a client's experience, like improving a passenger's seat on an aircraft

One business that offers proactive customer service is Kohl's. The store automatically emails consumers with tracking information and delivery updates once they place an online order. Kohl's notifies the consumer when their order will arrive if there is a delay. The consumer can avoid calling to find out the whereabouts of their package and when it will be delivered thanks to this approach.

Who takes the initiative separates proactive customer service from reactive customer care. Reactive service occurs when the client reaches out to the business first, whereas proactive service occurs when the business contacts the customer first.

It's like waiting for your houseplants to begin to wither before you water them—the damage is already done—to wait for a consumer to alert you to an issue. Even with a solution, the customer is probably already annoyed with your brand. By then, your team might find it difficult and time-consuming to tackle the issue.

Proactive customer care saves customers time and effort by foreseeing problems before they arise. For instance, a proactive method would be to notify customers via email or text message as soon as you know there will be a service interruption, as opposed to waiting for them to get in touch with you (reactive approach).

Despite the benefits of proactive customer care, no company can foresee every requirement that a customer may have. Combining the two is the optimal course of action: Determine which sectors can benefit from proactive customer service, then provide support by implementing reactive customer service.

It is impossible to exaggerate the value of taking the initiative to assist customers. Businesses trying to improve customer experiences must take a proactive approach to customer service.

89 percent of customers said they have had a pleasant surprise or positive experience from proactive customer support, per HelpLama research. Furthermore, positive experiences improve financial results: A favorable customer service encounter, according to 81% of consumers, makes them more likely to make another purchase.

It's like waiting for your houseplants to start wilting before you water them—waiting for a customer to alert you to a problem.

Understanding and anticipating the demands of your clients demonstrates to them how customer-focused your company is and how hard you work to provide an amazing experience. Long-term customer retention is higher when patrons feel valued and appreciated.

Proactive customer service's advantages: Here are some ways that your business can profit from proactive help.

- **Increased fidelity to the consumer**
  According to 67 percent of participants in Microsoft's Global State of Customer Service research, proactive customer service notifications are beneficial. You increase your chances of keeping consumers when you engage with them proactively.

Assume, for instance, that a client is stuck in traffic while traveling to the airport. The airline can proactively notify the customer that they will probably miss their flight because of their current position and offer suggestions for other flights. This kind of proactive customer care will maintain customers feeling satisfied and important while also increasing brand trust. You'll therefore witness increased client loyalty.

- **An Increase in sales:** Studies show that over 70% of internet buyers will back out of a transaction after adding an item to their cart. Furthermore, 17% of consumers will abandon their basket if they believe the checkout procedure to be excessively difficult. For this reason, to boost sales, proactive support and participation are required.

    A brief message from a customer support agent could encourage a hesitant customer to finish the transaction by helping them with an issue or providing an answer to a query. Proactive customer service and real-time communication have been shown by numerous businesses to increase sales. For instance, Spartan Race reported a 27% rise in retail sales and a 97% customer satisfaction rating via chat after introducing proactive help with AI-powered chatbots in their online store.

- **Less strain on assistance representatives:** The quantity of support tickets can be considerably reduced with proactive support. Proactively addressing frequently asked customer queries frees up team members to concentrate on the most urgent, complicated, and important support requests. Agents will therefore have more time and mental space to assist clients in finding genuine, personalized solutions to their difficulties. Because there will be fewer tickets, your agents will probably be more attentive and involved as well. This will improve worker happiness and satisfaction, which will have a good effect on how they arrive for work and interact with clients.

- **An increase in client satisfaction:** Proactively providing help results in enhanced client satisfaction and better experiences. Authors Bill Price and David Jaffee discuss how the greatest approach to delight customers is to eliminate the need for service in their book The Greatest Service is No Service. But to accomplish this, businesses need to offer proactive customer care. Businesses may generate great experiences by anticipating consumer pain points and making it unnecessary for customers to contact them. Everyone wins when clients don't have to get in touch with businesses to get assistance or information.

How your customer support department should be organized

Although the transition from reactive to proactive customer care may appear difficult, businesses that wish to outperform their competitors must make this change. This is how to provide prompt customer service.

- Communicate honestly with your clients.
- Conduct surveys regularly.
- Establish a knowledge foundation
- Observe your clients online
- Engage with your item
- Make use of technology
- Assemble the ideal group and give them authority
- Speak with your clients
- Instances of proactive customer service

Let's examine a few businesses that are enhancing the client experience by implementing proactive customer care tactics.

It's important to properly onboard customers, and there's always the first challenge of assisting them in learning about the benefits of your product or service. Providing advice and suggestions is a good method to interact with your clients and improve their experience.

For instance, before their first rental, new riders must complete a brief online course and test offered by Scoot. Subsequently, the organization sends out class reminders along with pointers and recommendations to help novice scooter riders overcome their fear of riding one for the first time.

One more illustration of outstanding onboarding and client service? Slackbot was developed by Slack to proactively interact and onboard new users.

Proactively supporting customers by offering guidance or a pertinent message in difficult situations is a great method to help them out.

Since Amazon is renowned for anticipating inquiries about delivery dates and times, it emails customers to let them know if there are any order delays. In addition, the corporation may provide the consumer a complimentary month of Amazon Prime membership as compensation for the inconvenience, all without the customer having to contact them. This facilitates better customer service and ensures that agents aren't overloaded with tickets about order delays and inquiries.

- **Reduce client annoyance**

It's critical to provide updates as they happen and to keep customers updated about any ongoing problems with the product, customer support, or operations. Let's say your business recently released a software upgrade. While it's wonderful for things to go smoothly, it's wiser—and more practical—to plan for any potential hiccups.

Customers of cloud service providers like DigitalOcean are renowned for receiving advance notice of system updates and disruptions, allowing users to make appropriate plans. Keeping users informed about changes and outages can help minimize customer complaints and save your support team time once an issue arises.

- **Inform clients when new products are released:**

Another method to interact with your viewership? Provide information about upcoming events, new features, goods, integrations, and styles.

For instance, when a new film from Cinemark is set to hit theatres, the corporation notifies a particular segment of its clientele by email who may find the film intriguing.

Zendesk employ messaging tools to send proactive, in-product messages to relevant customer segments that may be interested in attending webinars to increase webinar registration.

- **Take care of your clientele**

Building relationships with and keeping clients requires proactive customer interaction. You are fostering such relationships and gaining their trust when you provide recommendations, information, or best practices for using items to your consumers.

People are willing to utilize Apple products because they add innovative and fun elements to them and urge customers to get involved. For instance, Apple's "Shot on iPhone" initiative asked consumers to upload their best iPhone photos. The selected photos are displayed globally on billboards, on Apple's social media pages, and on the company's website.
Engaging your audience proactively with campaigns such as these fosters a greater sense of consumer loyalty and trust. above the

previous three years, Apple has maintained loyalty rates of above 90%, according to CIRP data.

- **Customers to upsell**

When you establish a solid rapport with your clientele, you may take proactive measures to prolong the buyer's trip by gently guiding them towards fresh and pertinent offers that are connected to previous purchases.

Deliveroo, for instance, raises the likelihood of ingredient add-ons by merely offering clients the choice before checkout.

Provide a customer with an upsell that solves a problem or satisfies their preferences based on their prior interactions with your business. Ideally, this will lead to a higher client retention rate. Put proactive customer service into practice right now.

Your organization, goods, and industry are all changing, review your communication strategies and customer service plans. More channels than ever exist for instantaneous consumer contact in the world of excellent customer service, including social media, messaging apps, live chat, mobile, and online.

You can meet the demands of your audience, solve issues before they arise, and make sure that crucial information is accessible with ease by providing proactive customer assistance and engagement.

Encouraging and engaging customers proactively can help you build long-lasting relationships, rather than leaving them on their own.

Predicting Consumers Needs Using Data and Feedback

To anticipate client demands through data and feedback, it is necessary to gather, evaluate, and act upon data from multiple sources. Businesses may provide better service and products by being proactive and able to predict what customers will want or demand in the future. This is how you do it: Monitor the goods and services that are bought, as well as how often and how much.

Record information about questions, grievances, and resolutions to find recurring problems and commonly asked questions. Track user activity on websites, including clicks, visits, time spent on pages, and patterns of navigation.

To learn more about customer experiences and expectations, use Net Promoter Score (NPS), customer satisfaction surveys (CSAT), and other feedback forms. Gather and examine user feedback from a range of platforms to learn about their thoughts and potential areas for development. Keep tabs on mentions, messages, and comments on social media sites to determine client sentiment and spot new trends.

Examine previous purchases to spot trends and forecast future purchasing behavior. Utilise information about what clients browse to gain insight into their preferences and future requirements. To learn about the preferences and interests of your customers, and observe how they interact with emails, content, and promotional materials.

To customize forecasts and communications, group clients according to age, gender, income, geography, and other demographic characteristics. Divide up your consumer base according to their involvement levels, usage habits, and purchasing habits.

Recognise reoccurring patterns and trends in customer feedback and behavior by utilizing data analytics technologies. Using past data, apply predictive analytics models to predict future requirements and behaviors of customers.

Recommendation Engines: Utilise machine learning algorithms to make product and service recommendations based on past browsing and purchasing behavior. Analyse customer reviews and comments using natural language processing (NLP) to determine sentiment and anticipate any problems.

Reacting to Information and Input

Develop marketing strategies based on anticipated needs and preferences that are specific to certain customer categories. Utilise consumer data to provide each individual with personalized discounts, promotions, and product recommendations.

Make use of data insights to create new features or products that meet unmet consumer demands or enhance current offers. Based on user input and usage data, continuously improve products and services. Inform clients ahead of time if information suggests problems may arise. Send out reminders and provide help, for instance, if a product normally requires maintenance after a specific amount of time. Educate customer support representatives on how to leverage data to offer individualized support. Give them details on the client's background and inclinations.

Create loyalty programs that reward regular customers and promote repeat business by utilizing data on consumer behavior. Using predictive analytics, identify at-risk consumers and put retention tactics in place like tailored outreach or exclusive incentives.

Make quick changes to tactics, goods, and services based on data that is available right now. Make sure that consumer feedback is taken into consideration and relayed back to them, demonstrating how their contributions result in observable advancements.

Instruments and Technologies

1. Customer Relationship Management (CRM) Systems: - Integration: To expedite data gathering and analysis, integrate all sources of customer data into a single CRM system.
- **Automation:** Automate data-driven marketing and customer care procedures with CRM technologies.

2. Analytics Platforms:- Data Visualisation: Make data patterns and insights easier to understand and act upon by visualizing them using analytics platforms.
- **Reporting:** Create reports regularly to monitor success against important metrics and modify plans as necessary.

3. Machine Learning and Artificial Intelligence (AI): - AI Tools: Use AI-driven tools for automated consumer interactions, predictive modeling, and advanced data analysis.

Systems for Machine Learning: Utilise machine learning to enhance customer insights and prediction accuracy over time.

Businesses can remain ahead of the curve and deliver superior service and products that meet and exceed customer expectations by leveraging data and feedback to foresee client demands. This proactive strategy fosters long-term profitability and loyalty in addition to improving consumer pleasure.

Chapter Five

The Little Things That Makes A Big Difference

The capacity to notice, evaluate, and understand even the smallest details of a work or circumstance is known as **attention to detail.** It is the skill of paying close attention to detail and being thorough. This ability goes beyond simply identifying errors; it includes a dedication to quality in all facets of your work, from the preliminary phases of planning to the completion of the task.

A person concentrating on paying close attention to details while using a computer for a project. The ability to pay close attention to detail is highly valued and has a big impact on job performance, career advancement, and overall organizational success. In the job, paying close attention to details is essential for the following reasons. Reducing mistakes and oversights, meticulous attention to detail enables you to consistently deliver high-quality work, which can have far-reaching effects across a variety of industries.

Establishing credibility and trust. Strong attention to detail demonstrates professionalism and a dedication to quality, which can help you gain the respect and confidence of stakeholders, supervisors, clients, and coworkers.

Increasing productivity and efficiency. By keeping an eye on the little things, you can spot any problems or bottlenecks before they become big ones. This can help you deal with problems faster and streamline procedures to increase production and efficiency.

Effective decision-making and problem-solving Paying close attention to details makes it easier to get and evaluate data, which is crucial for making decisions and addressing problems at work.

Five possible problems Being Faced by Employees who pay attention to detail

Although having a sharp eye for detail is a desirable skill, if it is not balanced appropriately, it can also cause problems. The following traps—which we like to refer to as **blind spots**—may present themselves to someone with an intense attention to detail:

- **Tunnel vision:** When you hyperfocus on small things, you risk losing sight of your goals and the big picture of your strategy.

- **Perception of micromanagement:** Putting too much effort into making every detail flawless could make you appear nitpicky or too controlling to others.

- **Feeling overwhelmed and immobile:** When everything appears equally important, you could feel overburdened and find it difficult to set priorities and go on.

- **Delayed start:** If you want to know everything up front, you might choose to postpone project start dates until all the specifics are worked out.

- **Never-ending refining:** Perfectionism can result in a never-ending cycle of changes, which makes it difficult to finish projects and go on.

However, in many positions, the benefits of having extraordinary attention to detail typically exceed these disadvantages. Furthermore, you can navigate these blind areas just by being aware of them.

Six indicators that you don't pay enough attention to detail

In many professions and sectors, failing to pay close attention to detail can have serious repercussions that affect both the caliber of your work and your success as a whole. If you think you might have trouble paying attention to detail, be aware of these warning indicators:

- **Regularly submitting incomplete work:** When submitting work, do you frequently forget to include attachments, skip over certain portions, or ignore crucial details? If you consistently turn in work that isn't fully completed, it's obvious that you're not paying enough attention to the details.

- **An ongoing requirement to correct errors:** You're not closely reviewing your work enough if it consistently returns to you with grammatical faults, omissions, or mistakes that need to be fixed.

Remarkable outcomes necessitate an acute attention to detail.

- **Putting speed ahead of accuracy:** Although efficiency is commendable, operating at a rapid speed all the time can lead you to miss important details. Should the word "fast" be the first one used to characterize your working style, you might be giving up precision in favor of speed.

- **Disregard for prior accomplishments:** You're not paying close attention to details throughout the process if you find yourself tearing your hair out over previous efforts because you can see so many errors or things you wish you'd done better.

- **Never the last person to evaluate something:** Your colleagues may not trust your editing abilities or your capacity to go over every detail before submitting the work if they routinely delegate the final review of shared projects to someone else.

- **Postponing minute details:** Saying "We'll worry about that later" in response to a complex inquiry suggests a propensity to put off crucial information until it's essential, which can result in mistakes and oversights.

Striking a balance is crucial, even while a deficiency in detail-oriented thinking could indicate a strength in strategic thinking. The first step to strengthening your attention to detail and producing flawless work is identifying these indicators.

What are some instances of detail-oriented behavior?

Let's check some instances of detail-oriented behaviour. A detail-oriented team member pointing out a detail to a fellow team member. A highly valuable soft talent that can greatly improve career development and job success is excellent attention to detail. When taking on challenging jobs, requires a methodical approach, organizational skills, and continuous vigilance. Finding minor spelling mistakes in emails or laboriously double-checking data and statistics in reports are just two examples of how attention to detail shows up in work that is of a higher caliber.

Persons with excellent attention to detail are known for their organizational abilities. Professionals with good organizational skills can prioritize work wisely, manage their time well, and meet deadlines with ease. This increases productivity and allows them to handle larger workloads. Attention to detail and efficient time management go hand in hand. Those who are strong in this area avoid procrastination, minimize stress, and maximize productivity to prioritize work, meet deadlines, and accomplish goals.

Strong analytical abilities are fuelled by attention to detail, which empowers professionals to precisely collect and understand data, spot patterns and trends, and exercise critical thought. These are especially important in positions requiring strong problem-solving and judgment skills. Being meticulous develops excellent observational abilities, which enable people to fully assess circumstances and spot trends. In business, these abilities are crucial for recognizing issues, seeing possibilities, and creating workable solutions.

Being an active listener is a crucial aspect of communication when showcasing attention to detail. Reducing misunderstandings and fostering smooth team collaboration can be achieved by giving your full attention, keeping eye contact, understanding, and remembering information throughout interactions.

Five amazing strategies to help you become more detail-oriented

The first step in improving your attention to detail is realizing how important it is. But how do you go about honing this ability? The following five amazing techniques will assist you in improving your ability to pay attention to the details:

- **Accept a deliberate pace.:** Slow down and put quality above quantity during your workday rather than approaching it like a mad dash. Incorporate regular breaks, inhale deeply, and give careful thought to the accuracy of your job. By breaking down difficult tasks into digestible chunks, time management strategies like the Pomodoro Technique can help you pay closer attention to detail.

- **Engage in single-tasking.:** Multitasking is a certain method to miss important details and a productivity killer. Strive to limit your distractions to one task at a time and get rid of social media, email, and multiple browser tabs. Task switching is regularly linked to increased error rates and shorter attention spans, according to research.

- **Put checklists and templates into practice:** If maintaining consistency proves to be difficult, make use of templates and checklists to make sure you always take care of the little things when working on complex projects. To ensure you don't miss any important details, create task-specific templates with checklists and pre-written email responses for frequent correspondence.

- **Ask for External/ others Feedback:** Feedback from others can be really helpful, particularly if you're still honing your attention to detail. Get a friend or coworker to proofread your work once you've finished it. They can offer new insights and point out any mistakes you might have overlooked.

- **Divide, prioritize up big tasks:** Overwhelmedness can cause you to rush things and miss important nuances. To combat this, divide large tasks into smaller, easier-to-manage parts. This method not only helps intimidating jobs seem more manageable, but it also offers frequent chances to review and concentrate on the finer points.

By putting these strategies into practice, you can sharpen your attention to detail, guarantee correctness and precision in your work, and set yourself up for success and professional advancement. Pay close attention to the interview questions and be ready to respond to them. Employers are eager to find out during a job interview whether the "detail-oriented" skill you described on your CV is accurate or overstated. To evaluate your actual level of attention to detail, they will be looking at several factors, such as:

How well you've studied the business, the position, and the job description; how effectively you've prepared intelligent questions that show you've paid attention to important facts. Being punctual demonstrates your regard for the interviewer's timetable.

The degree of specificity with which you address the questions, steering clear of imprecise generalizations in favor of thoughtful, well-thought-out examples. Your final inquiries demonstrate your interest in learning about the subtleties of the role and your attention to obtaining specific details.

In addition to these indicators, interviewers will probably ask specific questions to determine how much attention to detail you have, like:

"What systems do you have in place to check your work?" Having well-thought-out procedures shows that you are dedicated to precision. Providing concrete examples demonstrates your capacity to identify problems. "Tell me about a time when you caught an error or problem."

"Describe a project that requires a high level of accuracy." Give pertinent examples that highlight your ability to think critically and work meticulously. Providing a detailed approach highlights your attention to important preliminary aspects. "What are the first steps you take when starting a new project?"

Many of these are behavioral interview questions, which start with "Tell me about..." and are preferred by employers because they go beyond generalizations and let you give instances from real-world situations that demonstrate your abilities.

The Situation, Task, Action, and Result (STAR) method provides a useful structure for providing a thorough response while staying focused:

- **Situation:** Give the particulars of the situation.
- **Task:** Describe your tasks and role.
- **Action:** Describe your actions, stressing how attentive you were.
- **Result:** Whenever feasible, quantify the benefits that your vigilance has brought about.

For instance: "This happened while I was on the content team at CompanyXYZ (Situation). I was tasked with identifying our top traffic sources (Task). After meticulously analyzing our Google Analytics data, I discovered we had been misclassifying social ad traffic (Action). By updating the links, I clarified our sources, allowing us to better tailor our strategy and increase traffic by 15% (Result)." By strategically preparing and utilizing the STAR technique, you can demonstrate to interviewers that you possess an exceptional level of attention to detail, which is a crucial talent.

highlight on your CV your meticulous nature. In many different fields and occupations, where even the smallest mistake can have serious repercussions, attention to detail is crucial. Include the following in your CV as examples and real-world uses of attention to detail in the workplace:

- **Accounting and Finance**: To ensure accurate financial records, reconcile accounts, and identify errors or discrepancies that may result in costly mistakes or compliance issues, attention to detail is essential. "I prepared detailed monthly financial reports, statements, and forecasts with precise data entry, ensuring accuracy in calculations and compliance with accounting principles."

- **Medical Care:** Paying close attention to detail in the medical industry saves lives. Patient safety and high-quality care depend heavily on paying close attention to details, which includes anything from correctly interpreting diagnostic tests and giving medications to performing precise surgical procedures. "I developed and implemented a double-checking system for high-risk medications, reducing medication errors by 35% on the unit."

- **Construction and engineering**: To avoid costly mistakes and possible tragedies, attention to detail is crucial for guaranteeing the accuracy of blueprints, computations, and specifications as well as for adhering to safety procedures and building codes. "I identified and corrected a critical error in the foundation design for a high-rise project, preventing potential structural failures and saving the company an estimated US$500,000 in rework costs."

- **Legal profession:** In the legal industry, even the smallest mistake can have major repercussions for clients. For this reason, meticulousness is essential when creating contracts, interpreting rules and regulations, and creating legal documents. "I reviewed and analyzed contracts, statutes, and case law to identify relevant legal issues and precedents."

- **Sales and customer support:** Enhanced customer satisfaction and loyalty can be achieved by paying close attention to details throughout client encounters, getting to know their unique needs and preferences, and offering precise and tailored solutions. "I demonstrated in-depth knowledge of product features, specifications, and compatibility to assist customers in making informed purchasing decisions."

Paying attention to detail is essential to securing your ideal career. Your ability to pay close attention to detail can help you land the job of your dreams and advance your career. You can progress your career in any organization by comprehending its meaning, appreciating its value in the workplace, and actively cultivating and exhibiting this important soft skill.

Caring Handshakes and Individual Touches

A deeper emotional bond between your brand and your customers can be created through thoughtful gestures and personal touches that greatly improve the customer experience. Here's how to successfully include these elements:

1. **Customization**

   - **Using Customer Data - Customer Profiles:** Establish thorough profiles for your clients that include their data, purchasing history, and preferences.

Utilize this information to customize offerings and interactions.

2. **Customised Suggestions:** Provide recommendations for goods and services based on your browsing and past purchases. Customization demonstrates to clients your understanding of their requirements and tastes.

3. **Personalised Communications:** - Address by Name: In all correspondence, refer to consumers by name. A tiny gesture like this can add a personal and attentive touch to interactions.

4. **Personalised Notes:** On important events like birthdays, anniversaries, or holidays, send personalized notes. These could be straightforward well-wishes or exclusive deals and discounts.

5. Contemplative Motions

- **Handwritten messages:** Thank-You Cards: After making large purchases, give customers handwritten messages of appreciation. This small gesture can convey sincere gratitude and make a lasting impact.

- **Personal Messages:** Write notes accompanying purchases to thank clients for their purchase and to wish them pleasure using the product.

- **Surprise and Delight:** - Surprise: Occasionally, customers' orders come with little, surprises. This could be branded goods, a sample product, or a coupon for a discount on their subsequent purchase.

- **Exclusive Offers:** Give devoted customers early access to sales and new products, as well as exclusive discounts.

Give them a sense of appreciation and respect for their allegiance.

6. **Identifying Special Occasions:- Birthday Wishes:** On your clients' birthdays, send them personalized greetings and exclusive deals. They may feel cherished and remembered as a result of this action. During the festive seasons, send greetings and great offers. This can strengthen the brand's emotional resonance and foster favorable associations.

7. **Making Memorable Experiences**

- **Exceptional Service - Going the Extra Mile:** Educate and empower your employees to go above and beyond to help clients. Great service makes a lasting impression, whether it's by assisting customers in finding what they're looking for, offering comprehensive information, or promptly resolving a problem.

- **Further Enquiries:** Make follow-up calls to find out if consumers are happy with their purchases and to provide more help if required. This proactive demeanor may come across favorably.

- **Special Events:- Customer Appreciation Events:** Organise gatherings to express gratitude to your clientele. This could be a special class, an exclusive sale, or the unveiling of a new product.

- **In-Store Experiences:** Design distinctive in-store events, such as interactive displays, tasting events, or product demos. Positive associations and enduring memories can be formed with your brand through these events.

- **Personalised Packaging:-** Personalised Packaging: Make use of packaging that expresses the event or the customer's tastes. For instance, unique packaging for premium clients or special packaging for orders placed during the holidays.

Take note of the little things, like a branded label, an elegantly knotted ribbon, or environmentally safe materials, that go into packing. The unboxing experience may be improved by these additions. Actively seek out and pay attention to client input. This is known as **Active Listening.** Utilize these comments to enhance your goods and services and convey to clients how much you respect their input.

Interact with clients on social media by answering their questions, messages, and mentions. Express gratitude for compliments and quickly resolve any issues raised. Recalling Previous Clients: Identify and thank previous clients. Make sure they feel appreciated and rewarded by using loyalty programs.

Encourage a feeling of camaraderie among your clients by setting up channels for them to communicate with your company and one another. This might happen through forums, social media groups, or neighborhood gatherings. Provide staff members the freedom to decide for themselves and take action to improve the customer experience. More deliberate and individualized encounters can result from putting your trust in them to work in the customer's best interest.

Give credit to staff members who constantly provide outstanding customer service. This serves to both inspire people and reaffirm the value of kind deeds and intimate touches. You can create memorable experiences that encourage loyalty and strengthen the emotional bond between your customers and your company by adding kind gestures and personal touches to your customer encounters. Even though they are frequently insignificant, these initiatives can have a big impact on long-term business and consumer happiness.

Chapter Six

Going Above and Beyond

To deliver great customer service and encourage loyalty, satisfaction, and positive word-of-mouth, one must go above and beyond what is expected of them. This is known as going the extra mile. This chapter explores the concept of going above and beyond, going extra mile for customers, including real-world examples, company success stories, and doable advice for putting extra effort into your operations.

Businesses must embrace a customer-centric mentality that puts the wants, requirements, and welfare of their clients first if they want to genuinely go above and beyond. This strategy entails Recognising and projecting potential needs or desires of clients before they enquire.

Adapting communications and encounters to each client's unique tastes and background. Dealing with possible problems before they get out of hand and providing happy customers with remedies. Developing enduring, gratifying bonds with others via memorable and significant exchanges.

Example of Excellent Brands Customer Service

- **Zappos:-** Legendary Customer care. renowned for its customer-first philosophy, Zappos once had a customer care agent spend more than 10 hours on the phone making sure the customer's demands were satisfied. A key component of their company strategy is their dedication to customer service.

- **Free Returns and Quick Shipping:** Zappos provides customers with an easy and risk-free purchasing experience by offering a 365-day return policy along with free shipping in both directions.

- **Ritz-Carlton:-** Personalised Experiences: Staff members are educated to recall the preferences of visitors and customize their experience. For instance, when a visitor shares their favorite beverage or pastime, staff members will make every effort to include it in their stay. Employees can spend up to $2,000 per guest to fix any problem, which frees them up to deliver great service without having to wait around for red tape.

- **Southwest Airlines:-** amusing Flight Attendants: Southwest Airlines is well-known for its amiable and amusing flight attendants, who add to the enjoyable and unforgettable in-flight experience. As part of their dedication to providing convenient travel, Southwest permits customers to make changes to their itinerary without paying an additional price.

- **Nordstrom:** Even though Nordstrom does not sell tires, a client once brought a set of tires back to a Nordstrom location. The retailer put the needs of its patrons ahead of strict guidelines by accepting the return and issuing a refund.

- **Amazon:** - Customer-First Approach. Amazon is renowned for its policies that prioritize the needs of its customers. They demonstrate their awareness of client demands by extending their return window to accept gift returns over the Christmas season. Amazon showed their dedication to customer satisfaction by replacing the item, accelerating shipping, and sending a personal apology when a client's package was stolen.

- **Warby Parker:** - Home Try-On Program. This risk-free method of selecting the ideal pair of glasses lets clients try on up to five pairs at home before making a purchase. Warby Parker replaced a customer's glasses for free and added a thoughtful dog toy after the customer's dog chewed them up.

Set it as a goal to Provide staff members the freedom to decide in ways that will best serve customers without requiring management consent. They can deal with problems swiftly and efficiently because of their empowerment.

Invest in thorough training courses that educate staff members on how to spot chances to go above and beyond and deliver great customer service.

Get in touch with clients before problems arise. For instance, notify the consumer right away if a product is delayed and provide them with options or reimbursements. Find common problems and opportunities for development, gather and evaluate customer feedback regularly.

Make proactive improvements to the customer experience by using this information.

Tailor interactions based on consumer information. Remember client preferences, address them by name, and customize offers and messages to fit their needs. Get in touch with consumers to enquire about their happiness and to resolve any unresolved issues following a transaction or service encounter.

On occasion, astonish clients with modest but kind gestures like personalized notes of gratitude, complimentary samples, or exclusive offers. These unplanned kindnesses have the power to leave a lasting good impression. Send individualized greetings and exclusive incentives to commemorate significant client anniversaries or birthdays.

Organise extraordinary events that deliver your clients distinctive and unforgettable experiences. These could be invitation-only events, new product announcements, or neighborhood get-togethers. Involve clients with interactive events, workshops, or live demonstrations. These exchanges can strengthen ties with clients and increase their loyalty which in return helps to build a great Brand Business.

Chapter Seven

Using Complaints to Create Chances

Despite their common bad connotations, complaints provide businesses with priceless chances to strengthen their offerings, forge closer bonds with clients, and improve their reputation in general. Resolving concerns effectively can turn unhappy consumers into devoted supporters. This section explores methods for resolving grievances amicably, transforming bad events into good ones, and utilizing criticism to make improvements over time.

Pay attention to what the consumer is saying without interjecting. Express understanding and acknowledge their sentiments to demonstrate empathy. It can be helpful to support their feelings with statements like "I understand how frustrating this must be for you."

To make sure you comprehend the issue completely, make inquiries. This conveys to the client your sincere desire to help them find a solution. Take note of the grievance as soon as you can. Inform the client that their issue is being looked into, even if you can't solve it right away.

Give the consumer a deadline for the resolution and explain the activities you plan to take to address the problem. Accept responsibility for fixing the problem, even if it was brought on by uncontrollable circumstances. Do not point fingers or offer justifications. Say you're sorry in sincerity. Repairing a damaged relationship can be greatly aided by a heartfelt apology.

When it is possible, provide several solutions. This empowers the client and demonstrates your dedication to coming up with a solution that suits them. Make certain the steps are implemented as soon as promised. Confirm with the customer that the problem has been fixed to their satisfaction by following up.

Grant front-line staff the immediate ability to address typical issues. Delays are avoided, and it shows that you value client happiness. Make sure staff members have the tools they need to handle complaints by providing training on effective complaint handling.

Address Particular Issues. Craft your answer to specifically address the issues brought up by the client. Customers may feel devalued by generic responses. Express gratitude to the client for bringing the matter to your notice. This reaffirms your commitment to growth and your appreciation for their input.

Just and Proper remuneration that is just and suitable for the circumstances. This might encompass reimbursements, price reductions, or free goods or services. Occasionally, go above and beyond what the client anticipates. By doing this, a bad experience can be transformed into a memorable good one.

Ascertain whether the consumer is happy with the resolution by following up with them. This implies that you are interested in their continued experience. Take advantage of the chance to strengthen your relationship with the consumer by having follow-up conversations.

Testimonials from Customers. Tell tales of your successful complaint resolutions. This can show other clients how committed you are to providing exceptional service and help you gain their trust.

Honour and commend workers who manage complaints very well. This promotes a proactive culture of problem-solving.

Getting Better and Learning from Criticism

- **Complaint Analysis:** Review complaints frequently to spot reoccurring problems. You can use this to identify places that require development. Do a Root Cause Analysis to identify the underlying problems that give rise to complaints. This stops problems from happening again.

- **Implement Changes:** Make improvements to procedures, goods, or services based on the knowledge gathered from complaints. Policy, training, or operational procedure modifications may be necessary for this. Establish a mechanism for sending updates and enhancements to customers. This indicates that their opinions are taken into consideration and valued.

- **Assess Customer Satisfaction:** Survey customers both before and after modifications are implemented. This aids in evaluating how well your modifications are working. NPS Net Promoter Score can be used to determine how satisfied and loyal a customer is. Monitor changes in NPS to assess the effectiveness of your efforts to handle complaints.

Encourage staff members to contribute ideas for enhancing customer service and handling grievances to Cultivate a Culture of Continuous Improvement. This promotes involvement and a sense of ownership. Frequent training on handling complaints and best practices for customer service should be given. Provide staff with regular updates on new practices and advancements.

Disseminate the results of complaint analyses throughout the entire company. Openness promotes a culture of responsibility and ongoing development. Set measurable objectives to enhance customer happiness and decrease complaints. Monitor advancements and acknowledge successes.

Businesses may turn complaints into chances for development and improvement by responding to them politely, transforming bad experiences into good ones, and taking criticism to heart. This methodology not only augments client contentment but also cultivates a devoted clientele and a robust image for outstanding support.

Chapter Eight

Assessing and Enhancing Client Satisfaction

A successful firm depends critically on its ability to satisfy its customers. Businesses may ensure they are meeting and surpassing the demands and expectations of their consumers by tracking and enhancing customer satisfaction. The main measures for customer satisfaction, methods, and instruments for getting feedback, and procedures for continuous improvement are all covered in this chapter. **Net Promoter Score (NPS):** NPS calculates the chance clients will tell others about your company. Customers are asked to rate the chance on a scale of 0 to 10, and this information is divided into many categories.

Promoters (9–10): Loyal clients who are inclined to speak well about your company.

Passives (7-8): Contented but unenthusiastic clients who are susceptible to offers from rival businesses.

Detractors (0–6): Disgruntled clients who might put off future purchases from you.
  Subtraction % of Proponents - % of Distractors is NPS.

The Customer Satisfaction Score (CSAT) is a metric that expresses how happy customers are with a certain product, service, or encounter. Consumers use a scale, such as 1 to 5, to indicate how satisfied they are. CSAT is equal to (the total number of replies/sum of all ratings).

Customer Effort Score (CES) rates how simple it is to resolve customer issues and engage with customers. Consumers use a scale, such as 1 to 7, to rate the amount of effort needed. CES is equal to the (Total number of replies / (Sum of all effort scores)).

Retention Rate of Customers: - This indicator calculates the proportion of clients who stick with you over a given time frame. [(Number of customers at end of the period - Number of new customers during the period) / Number of customers at the start of the period] is the customer retention rate. muOne hundred.

Rate of Customer Churn: - The percentage of consumers who discontinue doing business with you over a given time frame is known as the churn rate. Customer Churn Rate is calculated as the total number of customers at the beginning of the period / Number of lost customers during the period) multiplied by 100.

First interaction Resolution (FCR):- FCR is a metric that expresses the proportion of customer concerns that are resolved during the initial interaction. FCR is equal to (total number of issues/number of issues handled on first contact) multiplied by 100

The term Customer Lifetime Value (CLV) refers to the estimation of a business's total revenue from a single customer account throughout the business relationship. Average purchase value average frequency of purchases average customer longevity equals CLV.

Surveys: - Online Surveys: To design and disseminate surveys, use tools like SurveyMonkey, Google Forms, or Typeform. **Email Surveys:** Use email surveys to obtain thorough responses. **On-app Surveys:** Include surveys for immediate feedback on your website or app.

Interviews with Customers:- One-on-One Interviews. Hold in-depth discussions to obtain qualitative understanding. Get a group of clients together to talk about their experiences and get feedback as a whole.

Social Media Surveillance:- Social Audio Instruments. Utilise applications such as

Hootsuite, Brandwatch, or Sprout Social to track and examine user reviews on social media sites.

Feedback Forms:- Use feedback forms to get feedback from visitors to your website. **Post-Purchase Forms:** After purchase, send feedback forms to learn about the customer's experience.

Interactions with client Service: Analysis of Call Centres: Examine contact center records to find recurring problems and client attitude. **Chat and Email Analysis:** Look at chat and email exchanges to find areas for improvement and feedback.

Automated NPS Tools:- Net Promoter Score (NPS): Utilise programs such as Wootric, Delighted, or Promoter.io to automate NPS surveys and monitor the results over time.

Client Testimonials and Stars:- Review Portals: Keep an eye on client testimonials on Yelp, Google Reviews, and Trustpilot.

Ratings for Products: Examine reviews on online retailers such as Amazon to determine how satisfied customers are.

Procedures for Continuous Improvement

Regular Feedback Analysis:- To keep an up-to-date grasp of client satisfaction, continuously gather feedback from a variety of sources. To identify recurring problems and opportunities for development, look for trends and patterns in the feedback.

Actionable Insights:- Root Cause Analysis. Examine the fundamental causes of consumer complaints and discontent by conducting root cause analysis. Set issues in order of importance according to how they will affect client satisfaction and company performance.

Implement Changes:- Process Improvements. Apply modifications to services, goods, or processes in response to input. Employees should receive continual training to close any gaps found and enhance interactions with customers.

Monitor and Measure:- Performance indicators. Track important indicators related to customer satisfaction over time to assess the effects of improvements that have been made. Establish a feedback loop to let customers know about updates and improvements and to let them know you respect their input.

Involvement of Customers:- Advisory Boards for Customers: Form advisory boards with devoted patrons to get opinions and recommendations regularly. To obtain early input and make required adjustments, include customers in beta testing new features or products.

Recognition and Awards:- Recognise Employees: Honour staff members who go above and beyond to increase client happiness. This fosters a customer-centric culture and inspires the staff. Express gratitude to clients with customized thank-you messages or exclusive deals for their insightful input.

Businesses may improve client experiences, encourage loyalty, and propel long-term success by assessing customer satisfaction through key indicators, obtaining feedback using a variety of tools and strategies, and putting continuous improvement procedures into place.

Chapter Nine

Using Technology to Provide Better Service

In the digital age we live in today, technology is essential to how businesses shape consumer experiences and can provide better customer service. Businesses may improve customer interactions, expedite procedures, and deliver individualized experiences that either match or surpass customers' expectations by skilfully utilizing technology.

Use technology to improve the customer experience, and stress the significance of striking a balance between technology and human interaction. CRM programs such as HubSpot, Salesforce, or Zoho CRM enable companies to centrally store and handle all customer data and interactions. This makes it possible to see the customer from all angles, allowing for more informed and individualized service.

CRMs make communication easier by keeping track of customer interactions over a variety of channels. This guarantees that customers, no matter who they communicate with within the organization, receive pertinent and consistent responses.

offer a smooth customer experience, omnichannel support combines many communication channels (such as phone, email, live chat, social media, and in-app messaging). Clients can change channels without losing the context of their exchanges. Chatbots and live chat technologies allow for real-time support, cutting down on wait times and raising customer satisfaction.

Customers may track orders, retrieve information, handle their accounts, and take care of problems on their own with the help of mobile apps and customer portals. Customers are empowered as a result, and fewer in-person interactions with customer support are required. By leveraging user data, mobile apps can improve the entire user experience by offering tailored offers, notifications, and suggestions.

AI-powered predictive analytics can foresee client preferences and needs, enabling companies to proactively present goods or solutions to clients before they even become aware of their needs. Artificial intelligence (AI) can assess client sentiment by analyzing social media mentions and customer comments. This allows organizations to resolve problems before they become more serious.

Utilizing VR and AR technology can improve virtual tours, product demos, and customer service. Before making a purchase, shoppers can use augmented reality (AR) to see how a product might look in their house. Virtual reality (VR) may be utilized for remote assistance, giving clients visual instructions on how to set up or troubleshoot products. This increases the efficiency of customer care.

Tools for Automation and Personalisation

Chatbots and Virtual Assistants: Chatbots offer round-the-clock assistance, responding to typical client questions and managing repetitive duties devoid of human involvement. Intelligent chatbots make use of natural language processing (NLP) to comprehend and provide tailored answers to consumer questions. Additionally, they can refine their responses over time by taking lessons from previous exchanges.

Email Marketing Automation: Companies can divide their audience into groups according to their purchasing patterns, behavior, or preferences by using email automation platforms like ActiveCampaign or Mailchimp. Customers will be guaranteed to receive material that is relevant to their interests thanks to this. To increase consumer engagement and loyalty, automation can send out customized emails in response to particular events, such as birthdays, recent purchases, or abandoned carts.

Personalisation Engines: Personalisation engines make use of user data to present material that is tailored to the interests, actions, and locations of individual users. This can include specific discounts, customized content for websites and applications, or recommendations for products that are unique to each user. By using these tools, organizations can create customized experiences for every touchpoint, from the first point of contact to the follow-up after a purchase.

Customer input and Survey Tools: Businesses may get real-time input from customers at important junctures in their journey by using tools such as Medallia, Qualtrics, or SurveyMonkey. This facilitates quick fixes and maintains client satisfaction. By combining AI with feedback systems, it is possible to analyze replies for sentiment and pinpoint specific areas in which customers are happy or unhappy.

Loyalty and Rewards Programs: Thanks to technology, loyalty programs can be automated so that customers can receive discounts, points, or prizes based on their brand engagement or purchasing behavior. Make the program more relevant and interesting for every user by using consumer data to customize loyalty rewards to specific preferences.

Harmonizing Human Touch and Technology

Automation is effective, but it's crucial to keep a human touch in interactions with customers. A more human connection can be established by adding the customer's name, past exchanges, and customized preferences to automated messaging.

Teach AI systems to discern when human intervention is required, such as in intricate or highly sensitive circumstances. When necessary, chatbots ought to be able to easily escalate a problem to a human agent.

Make sure that human agents are accessible for more delicate or complex issues, but use technology to handle regular inquiries. When addressing more complex issues, customers value having an actual conversation with a representative. Teach customer care agents to be empathetic, sympathetic, and emotionally intelligent, particularly when handling complaints or issues that call for a more nuanced response.

Guarantee a seamless handoff between automated systems and human representatives. To save the consumer from having to repeat themselves, whenever a chatbot transfers a conversation to a live agent, the agent ought to have access to the chat history. Give customer support representatives the resources they need to co-browse or provide video support with clients. This blends the personal touch of in-person communication with the effectiveness of technology.

While some customers favor digital engagement, others favor face-to-face communication. Give clients the choice to communicate via the method of their choice while honoring their choices. Ask your customers about how they interact with your brand through technology regularly. Utilize these suggestions to fine-tune and enhance the ratio of automation to human interaction.

Both technology and client demands are changing quickly. Keep an eye on the success of your technology-driven service initiatives at all times, and be prepared to make adjustments in response to client input and new developments. Make sure that your technology is always improving, not worsening, the user experience by utilizing a cycle of testing, feedback, and modification.

Businesses may provide outstanding service that delights customers and builds long-term loyalty by strategically employing technology to enhance the customer experience, automating and personalizing interactions, and keeping a balance with the human touch.

Chapter Ten

Staying Ahead of Industry Trends

Customer retention is a good indicator of how well your current customers are satisfied with both your product and level of service. Additionally, it's essential to the majority of subscription-based businesses and service providers.

A perfect world would have a 100% retention rate. In actuality, though, a "good" proportion differs depending on the industry. For small enterprises, the standard is typically in the range of 20 percent. E-commerce companies should have a rate higher than 35 percent.

According to the most recent survey, the average retention rates for the following industries are broken down: Industry percentages for retention

- Professional services: 83%; media 84%
- Transportation and automobiles 83%
- **Insurance** 83%
- 81% IT, 80% Construction
- 78% in finance
- 78% in Telecommunications
- 77% in healthcare
- 77% of software
- 75 percent of banking

Spending large sums of money on marketing, advertising, or sales outreach doesn't always make sense because firms that value their connections with current clients are typically the ones that see long-term success.

Given that former consumers have already established trust in your brand and may even have developed a rapport with your sales and support team, it is simpler to convert them into repeat customers and maintain high revenues. Furthermore, satisfied customers are more inclined to promote your business in their neighborhood, creating free publicity for you.

Enhancing the client experience is the key to increasing customer service retention. Indeed, according to 77 percent of consumers polled for the most recent Zendesk Customer Experience Trends Report, they are more devoted to businesses that provide excellent customer service when problems occur.

Seventy-two percent are prepared to pay extra for a business that provides positive client experiences. Furthermore, half of them state that they place a higher value on the client experience now than they did a year ago.

These tactics will help you deliver a great client experience and encourage repeat business.

Provide multichannel customer assistance to meet clients where they are. Support via omnichannel is a great way to keep customers. Agents can provide highly customized experiences by using contextual information about clients from multiple platforms.

It not only makes conversational sales and support strategies possible, but it also improves customer experience (CX). Customers may interact with a person on the platform of their choosing and get faster resolutions when firms offer omnichannel assistance.

Quickly address customer service inquiries. Research indicates that customers are more satisfied when initial responses are sent quickly. In our 2021 CX Trends Report, 73% of respondents stated that quick support resolutions are essential to a positive customer experience.

Faster resolutions should ideally follow quicker responses. You should still reply to customers as soon as possible, even if you are unable to resolve their issues right away.

A brief note informing the client that you have received their inquiry can serve as a prompt response. Better still, give them an approximate time frame for problem resolution.

If customers are aware that you're actively working towards a solution, they will be more patient; it helps to make clear expectations on the timeline upfront.

Customise communications with support personnel. When they are repeatedly asked to explain a problem, customers become irritated. Repeated, tiresome interactions also increase the likelihood that customers will walk out.

Give agents the resources they require in a customer support system so they can quickly access customer data, review previous exchanges, and expedite interactions. For instance, the Zendesk Agent Workspace provides agents with client context so they can provide a customized experience.

Provide a loyalty incentive: Increase customer retention by rewarding clients who are loyal to your company. Customers will be more likely to stick around if you show them you value their company in addition to your excellent product.

To purchase consumer loyalty for your company, think about providing: Programs for loyalty, coupons for discounts, special deals, VIP gatherings, Early-access advantages

Loyalty programs come in several forms, ranging from tiered benefits to point-based schemes. These rewards aid in gathering comprehensive client information, enabling your company to provide more individualized communications and experiences.

Provide a program for referrals: Create an effective referral program in five easy steps. Referral programs help with both acquisition and customer retention simultaneously. This word-of-mouth marketing tactic works well since it attracts new customers who are already confident in your company because they heard from a reliable source.

Additionally, it strengthens relationships with current clients who gain more advantages from doing business with you and promoting your brand. Several well-liked rewards consist of: Money, Free merchandise or goods, Give store credit. By encouraging consumers to return, offering these incentives will help your firm. Additionally, the social evidence that devoted customers provide will give it a competitive edge.

Make sure workers have a good experience. Contented staff members are typically more likely to offer the best possible customer service and build enduring bonds with customers that increase customer retention. Encouraging employees to establish relationships can have a significant impact on fostering trust and retaining consumers, even in the event of problems.

Lowering attrition rates is another benefit of fostering a healthy work environment. This is advantageous to your company since employees who stay on longer are more likely to be knowledgeable and sensitive to the needs of your clients.

Regularly get client feedback. One of the most effective strategies for lowering churn rates and improving client retention is customer feedback. Direct feedback from your clients is helpful if you want to know what is and isn't working for them.

Conduct surveys to give your customers a voice. Simple customer satisfaction surveys that ask for a "thumbs up" or "thumbs down" once a ticket is resolved are a great idea, but it's especially helpful to include more detailed questions like these: What would you say about your usage of our product? For you, what isn't working, and why?

Which of these channels would you rather use for customer service? Include input from members of your customer service team in your surveys as well. Since they are closest to the clientele, they can recognize typical grievances and inclinations.

Establish a robust clientele. Establish an online community where devoted clients can communicate and exchange stories. Customers can use this as an instructional platform to learn more about your products, and it provides you with a direct line of communication for their concerns and ideas.

Engaging with consumers in virtual environments such as these enables you to promptly resolve issues and maintain long-term customer loyalty.

Six instances of client retention and their efficaciousness

Retaining customers is essential for success. Don't, however, just believe what we say. Here are some examples of how well-known companies are prioritizing retention in the real world.

1. Offer a seamless online experience (Amazon). Meeting client expectations is one of the simplest instances of a customer retention strategy. Consumers now demand online experiences that are either as good as or better than those they receive in person. 65 percent of customers want to buy from companies that offer quick and easy online transactions, according to our 2021 Trends Report. And 49 percent awarded Amazon the highest scores for service for that reason.

2. Make every consumer feel like a VIP (Four Seasons). Luxurious hotels are well known for their superior, upscale guest services. The Four Seasons uses a blend of cutting-edge technology and personalized attention to provide every guest with an even greater sense of luxury. When it comes to any questions or requests for assistance, including restaurant recommendations and reservations, room service orders, arrival or early checkout, and even private jet reservations, guests can use Four

Seasons Chat to message staff via platforms like WhatsApp.

3. Create sympathetic connections with customers (Zappos) If there's one thing about customer service abilities you should be aware of, it's that developing enduring relationships with customers requires empathy. Our 2021 CX Trends Report shows that 49% of clients desire agents to have empathy. Zappos launched a hotline during the pandemic so that users could contact or speak with a support agent about anything, including the newest Netflix series.

4. Take the initiative (Dolar Shave Club). Consumers look to brands to anticipate their needs and address problems before they arise. For this reason, providing proactive service is crucial to keeping clients. A chatbot is available to greet users of the Dollar Shave Club website and respond to frequently asked queries, saving customers from contacting customer service or leaving their cart unfinished.

5. Promote causes that your clients are interested in (Bombas) According to our 2021 CX Trends Report, 54% of consumers prefer to purchase goods from businesses that place a high priority on diversity, equity, and inclusion in their communities and workplaces, and 63% prefer to purchase goods from businesses that practice social responsibility. Aware of this, Bombas provides a piece of clothing with every transaction to a charity that deals with homelessness or shelters.

6. Use Polaris to create a unified customer view. Our 2022 CX Trends Report states that 73% of business executives believe there is a direct correlation between customer service and business performance. By building a single customer view, you can empower agents to give your clients richer, more customized experiences. By using robust support software to provide best-in-class help across multiple channels and boost agent productivity by 30 to 40 percent, Polaris hopes to keep its loyal customers.

The goal of customer retention strategies and initiatives is to maintain a client's relationship with your business and motivate them to make additional purchases. Several well-liked customer retention programs consist of: VIP programs, Programs for loyalty, Reward programs

Although establishing a solid reputation for your business and a devoted clientele takes time, with perseverance and effective customer support software, you'll be much closer to winning over your clients' trust. To communicate with customers, use Zendesk. You'll be even closer to creating a customer experience that people will rave about with cutting-edge customer service capabilities like omnichannel connectivity, integrated support, and AI-powered productivity tools.

Businesses can create enduring customer loyalty through the application of these tactics, which not only keep customers but also transform them into ardent brand promoters. Building a consumer base that sticks with your business over time requires nurturing emotional ties, acknowledging loyalty, and continuously providing outstanding value.

Chapter Eleven

Case Studies and Success Stories

Customer Service's Future

Remaining competitive in the face of evolving trends and developments in customer service is imperative for businesses. Customer expectations, which are constantly evolving, along with technological advancements—particularly in the areas of automation and artificial intelligence—will influence the future of customer service.

This chapter looks at new developments in customer service, the expanding use of automation and artificial intelligence, and how companies can get ready for the rising expectations of their clients.

Clients need a smooth and consistent experience from businesses on social media, over email, over the phone, and during in-person meetings. For businesses to offer a unified and consistent consumer experience, these channels must be integrated.

By tracking customer interactions across all channels, unified customer profiles let organizations provide personalized and contextually relevant service. Regardless of the channel they use, this comprehensive understanding of the customer guarantees that their demands are served effectively.

Real-time support alternatives like live chat, chatbots, and video calls are becoming standard as the desire for quick fixes increases. To satisfy client expectations, businesses need to be prepared to offer prompt support. With the growth of Internet shopping and international marketplaces, round-the-clock customer support has become essential. To guarantee 24/7 availability, businesses are embracing automated technology and international support teams more and more.

Businesses can provide extremely customized client experiences because of developments in data analytics. Businesses can customize offers, recommendations, and communications to each customer's unique tastes and actions by utilizing customer data.

This goes beyond simple personalization by utilizing AI and machine learning to forecast client demands and provide tailored solutions instantly. By predicting needs and making pertinent recommendations, this strategy improves the client experience.

Businesses are expected to align their processes with eco-friendly and ethical standards as consumers prioritize sustainability. This entails providing environmentally friendly products, cutting waste, and being open and honest about the effects on the environment. Brands that show a dedication to environmental and social problems are attracting more and more attention from consumers. Customer service techniques that integrate corporate social responsibility (CSR) can enhance brand loyalty and draw in socially concerned customers.

Preventive customer engagement is contacting customers before problems occur. Businesses can use predictive analytics to find possible issues and fix them before they negatively affect the consumer experience. Providing value-added services keeps clients interested and improves their overall brand experience. Examples of these services include personalized tips, reminders, and exclusive content.

By offering prompt answers to frequently asked questions, chatbots powered by artificial intelligence are transforming customer service. These bots can manage many requests at once, freeing up human agents to work on more complicated problems.

As a result of client interactions, sophisticated AI chatbots can learn and become more adept at comprehending and answering queries. Through continuous learning, chatbots can eventually offer more precise and beneficial support.

Routine customer service duties like order tracking, appointment scheduling, and account administration are increasingly being handled by automation. Businesses can cut expenses and increase efficiency by automating these procedures. Automated processes can direct client questions to the right division or representative, guaranteeing prompt and effective resolution of problems. Wait times are shortened, and the whole customer experience is improved.

AI-powered instruments can find patterns and trends in enormous volumes of customer data. Businesses may anticipate client wants, tailor products, and enhance service delivery with the help of this information.

Businesses may assess customer happiness and take proactive measures to address unfavorable comments by utilizing AI to analyze client sentiment in real time. This promotes client loyalty and preserves a favorable brand image.

Customer service is changing as speech assistants like Apple's Siri, Google Assistant, and Amazon's Alexa gain traction. Voice-activated support can be used by businesses in their customer care strategy to provide convenient, hands-free help. With NLP, artificial intelligence (AI) systems can comprehend and reply to consumer questions in conversational, natural language. By improving the intuitiveness and human-likeness of interactions with AI systems, this technology improves the user experience.

Businesses must continue to be flexible and adaptive due to the rapid growth of technology and changes in consumer behavior. Businesses that can adapt swiftly to new technological developments and shifting consumer demands will have a greater chance of success.

Companies should fund their customer service teams' ongoing education and training. Keeping up with the most recent methods, instruments, and consumer preferences guarantees that staff members are prepared for any obstacles down the road.

Including clients in the process of creating new goods and services can result in innovations that are more tailored to their requirements. Co-creation guarantees that offerings are appealing to the intended audience and develops a closer relationship with clients.

Companies should embrace an experimental approach, putting new concepts to the test and making adjustments in response to input from clients. This strategy enables firms to remain ahead of changing client expectations and promotes continual improvement.

Ensuring data privacy and security is crucial because organizations depend more and more on data to improve customer service. Consumers anticipate responsible and open handling of their information by businesses.

Even while automation might increase productivity, retaining a human element in customer service is crucial for fostering relationships based on trust and empathy. To offer a better customer experience, businesses need to strike the correct balance between technology and interpersonal communication.

Companies should make investments in the newest technology for customer service, such as automation, artificial intelligence, and data analytics, to remain competitive. These resources can assist businesses in staying ahead of the curve and providing top-notch service.

Navigating the challenges of the future will require a culture of adaptability and resilience. Companies that cultivate an inventive, adaptable, and customer-focused culture will be better positioned to satisfy changing consumer demands.

Customer service has a bright future ahead of it because of new developments and trends that offer creative methods to wow clients and create enduring bonds. Businesses can make sure they not only meet but also surpass client expectations in the future by utilizing AI and automation, adopting customer-centric strategies, and planning.

Conclusion

Final Thoughts

It's important to review the main ideas covered in this book as we draw to a close our final discussion into the art of satisfying and exceeding consumer/ customer expectations. Exceeding expectations is a journey that calls for ingenuity, hard work, and a sincere desire to provide great service at every turn.

Knowing What to Expect from Customers. Great customer service is rooted in a thorough comprehension of what clients anticipate from your company. These expectations are influenced by individual preferences, industry norms, and prior experiences. You may lay the groundwork for enduring customer relationships by acknowledging and meeting these expectations.

Building a Culture of Great Service. Promoting a culture of great service requires a customer-centric mindset. Giving your team the tools they need to succeed—training, defined expectations, and capable leadership—will guarantee that every encounter demonstrates your dedication to quality.

Anticipating Customer requirements. Predicting and attending to customers' requirements before they even come up is the essence of proactive customer care. Through the use of data, feedback, and personalization, enterprises may craft customized experiences that truly connect with their clientele.

The customer experience can be enhanced by small yet impactful activities such as thoughtful gestures, attention to detail, and generating memorable moments. These are the Little Things That Make a Big Difference. These components set your brand apart and provide consumers with a positive first impression.

Going the Extra Mile. Companies that regularly go above and beyond to surprise and please their clients are considered exemplary. By going above and above what is expected of you, you not only cultivate customer loyalty but also establish a standard for what constitutes excellent service.

Transforming Complaints into Opportunities. Managing client complaints diplomatically and transforming bad experiences into favorable results is an essential competency. These unsatisfactory situations can be turned into chances for development, enhancement, and improved client connections.

Measuring and Enhancing Customer Satisfaction. Sustaining high levels of customer satisfaction requires ongoing improvement. Businesses may evaluate their performance and make the required improvements to improve the customer experience by utilizing measurements, tools, and feedback loops.

Using Technology to Provide Better Service. Customer service is being revolutionized by the integration of technology, from automation and artificial intelligence to data analytics. Technology may improve efficiency and personalization while maintaining a human touch, which will result in better service outcomes.

Cultivating Long-Term Customer Loyalty. Consistent, tailored encounters that foster emotional bonds are the foundation of long-term loyalty. Acknowledging and thanking devoted clients strengthens these relationships and promotes ongoing participation.

Getting Ready for Customer Service's Future. New developments in technology, changing consumer expectations, and developing trends will all influence the future of customer service. To succeed in this changing environment, businesses need to prioritize ethical behavior, stay flexible, and make innovative investments.

Exceeding customer expectations is a journey that takes time and requires a sincere dedication to quality work. Every conversation you have with a client is an opportunity to show how committed you are to giving them great service. Adopting the values presented in this book can help you motivate your staff to continuously aim for excellence and leave a lasting impression on your clients.

It's time to get out on your quest to exceed client expectations. Regardless of your role—business owner, team leader, or customer service specialist—the ideas and tactics covered here offer a path to success. Recall that continuously exceeding expectations rather than just meeting them is the actual test of great service.

As you proceed, remember to put your clients first in all you do. Pay attention to what they need, anticipate what they want, and always be prepared to go above and beyond. By doing this, you'll develop a brand that stands out for its dedication to excellence in addition to gaining the loyalty of potential clients. Your company may become a shining example of great service by taking the first step on your journey to exceeding expectations.

Acknowledgement

My sincere gratitude goes out to my family and friends for their continuous support and inspiration along this trip. With special gratitude to each and everyone for their contributions, as well as to my mentors and coworkers for their priceless advice and insights and my amazing readers. Without each of you, this book would not have been possible.

Thank you so much.

If you Enjoy this copy, you can as well get my other book:

- **How to start A Business For Beginners 2024**: (Turn Your Company Into a Money Machine and Earn a Profit with your Business (Starting your Dream Business)

www.ingramcontent.com/pod-product-compliance
Lightning Source LLC
Chambersburg PA
CBHW071926210526
45479CB00002B/567